SIMON'S MASTERPIECE

One day in a prison, Simon, The Pitcher, a prisoner, pitched, as he always did, against both sides. One day no one on either side got a hit.

James S. LaVilla-Havelin

Photographs By Richard Margolis

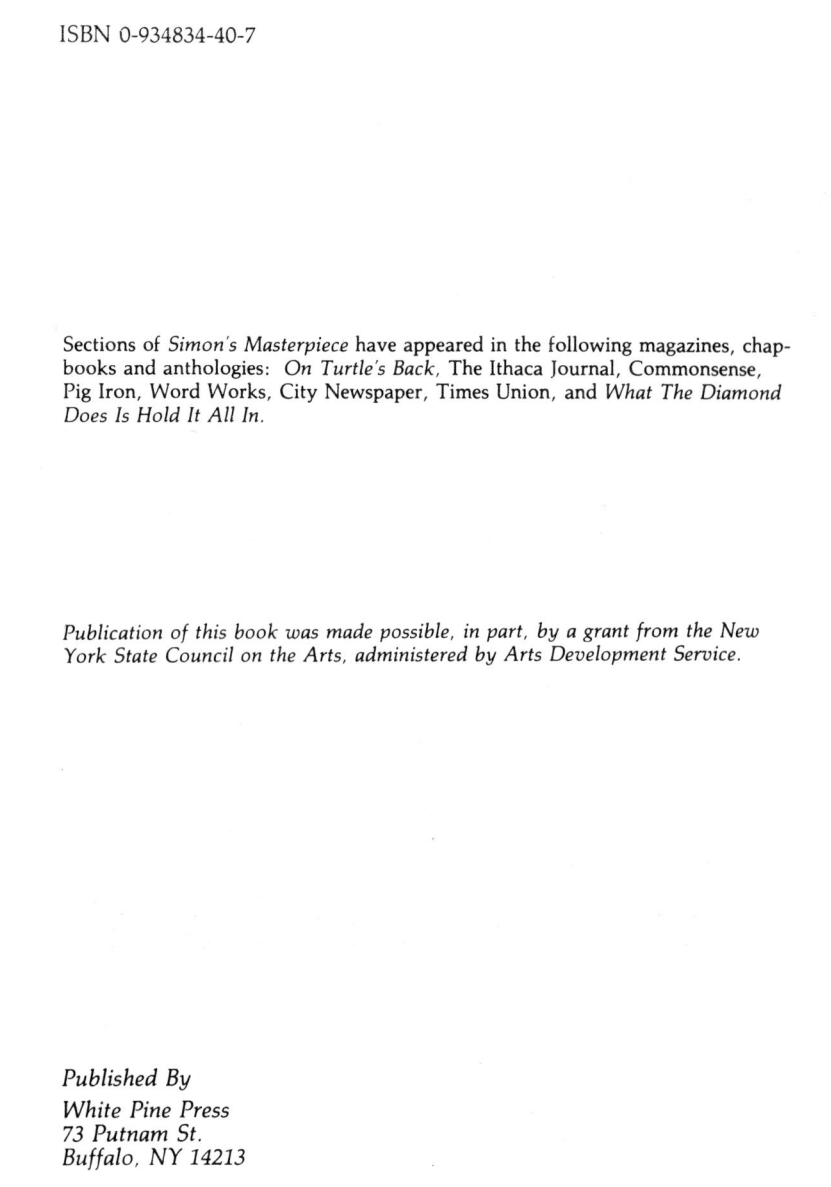

© 1979, 1983 James S. LaVilla-Havelin

ISBN 0-934834-40-7

Sections of *Simon's Masterpiece* have appeared in the following magazines, chapbooks and anthologies: *On Turtle's Back,* The Ithaca Journal, Commonsense, Pig Iron, Word Works, City Newspaper, Times Union, and *What The Diamond Does Is Hold It All In.*

Publication of this book was made possible, in part, by a grant from the New York State Council on the Arts, administered by Arts Development Service.

Published By
White Pine Press
73 Putnam St.
Buffalo, NY 14213

there is dreaming
and there is this stretch and kick and fire
perfect
       in there, in there
swaying on the small hill the mound is

in this sleep of perfection
it all slows down
it quiets to a whisper
and they watch

they watch him fool them
they watch their bats
                not get around on him

they watch what is perfect
and exhausting and empty

scoreboard empty
one man's triumph
the kind of quiet
the kind of perfect
                that leaves them shaking
                their heads

as if
they
were
dreaming

Think of the land
Cherry Valley to Syracuse

Syracuse to Rochester

Rochester to Buffalo

Erie, Lackawanna

land darkening, land levelling off

canal land, the deep swaths glacier-cut
    of lakes

vineyard land

Think of the land
levelling off
Rochester to Buffalo
to the airless, flat, pushed-down land
where the castle-darkened-prison-wall
rises
       makes shadows,   stands

think of the land —
Simon
saw mostly only cells:
an Ohio prison
a Pennsylvania prison
a gang in Georgia where he got the long scar
that runs as straight as Route 20
Cherry Valley to Syracuse to Rochester to Buffalo
across his cheek

Think of the land
and forget the man who is the legend
that this poem is about

the man, struggling in the dark
on an airless plain;   think
of the land, of the night run its course
from Lackawanna's glowing steel mill darkness
to the salt beach at Nauset

caught between the fire and the sea
slave, prisoner, in this grey no man's land

Think of the land
it is part of the story, too

Porter was cleaning out his desk and going home.
I was writing up the Yankee game we had just seen, a tepid affair,
characteristic of the Yankees of the early seventies.

Sometimes I wondered if it wasn't that all of us, even the people
who weren't Yankee fans, felt a loss of glory and a simple failure
to heed the lessons of the past, the magnificent Yankee past.

Mostly, I just watched them, game to game, travelling a few times
a year up to Syracuse to check out the young prospects;
wondering if even the whole Yankee era was something out of baseball
that was gone now, forever.

Porter and I would be going to the bar in a few minutes.
Dusty afternoon air filled the office.
Everything I knew about sports reporting, I had learned from Porter.

And you should have heard him talk about the old days, riding the trains
with the ballplayers...
Stories
        stories...

Porter was cleaning out his desk and going home.
He called over to me as I cracked out the game-winning hit in the third
Inning on my old typewriter,
                "Hey, kid, you going upstate in a couple of days?"
"Yeah, Porter... Hall of Fame inductions."
"Well, take this thing..."
                And he tossed me a baseball.

It was a regulation hard ball, with a signature on it.
I gripped it tight. I think there is a bit of pitcher in each of us —
Gripping like that, imagining the one pitch near the end of a World Series.

Most autograph balls are new balls, they haven't been scuffed and tattered
by play. But this ball looked like it had lasted a whole season.
And it had written on it in a scrawl,
                simon 27403

Porter came over to my desk, a shoebox under his arm, and his personal files
stuffed helter skelter in a bulging briefcase.
He saw that I was wondering about the ball, and the name, and he simply said,
"Check the files."

We left the office in the August heat.
No wonder ballplayers wilt in this, I thought, remembering teams that had
faded almost beyond memory in Augusts past.

Porter looked back once, and repeated, slowly to me,
"Look him up, kid. Look Simon up."

We went down to drink. Drink and stories and the ball game

We all play, over and again in our minds — with perfect plays
and perfectly amazing play, and the symmetry of grass and walls and number

Porter looked back once, and then walked out.
He looked more like an old man than he ever had,
And I wasn't "Kid" any longer...

The man in the wheelchair was playing electric darts.
His head would bob in a motion half-uncontrolled
    and half to the timing of the ticking circuits
       of the game.
He had the timing down

Sun danced over bottles behind the bar.

In perfect green, the diamond on the screen —
A black box above the door of the bar —
The Yankee game.

Two men at the end of the bar were arm wrestling.
Their bodies tense, their muscles straining.

If you looked out the front window of the bar —
It was a long narrow bar with a small street
        window —
All you could see was the prison wall.

Sitting on a barstool near the middle of the bar
You could not even see the top of the wall.
Just a wall, stone, sunlight even on it.

The man in the wheelchair won another game,
Motioned to the bartender for another beer
And bobbed again, stutter-fear-bobbing —
The head ringing, and the spine frozen.

The Yankee defense was giving the game away.
All the tension in the bar was in the elbows
of the men who were arm wrestling.

It was hot and August and their foreheads
were soaked. Sweat dripped in their eyes.
Their shirts stuck to their bodies.

A cheap hit cost the Yankees a run.
I took out my handkerchief, wiped my
forehead, my neck, took a pull off my
bottle of Black Horse, and turned to the
bartender,

"You know where I can find Bill Walters?"

Just as he was about to point,
The voice came from the bobbing head,
its words in spitting thrusts —

"I'm   him   what do   you   want?"

He won another dart game.
The Yankees stranded two men.
And I sat down next to Walters —

"Warden tells me you knew Simon."

His eyes were empty. Pain or time or
no reason — empty.
And he smiled.

"Sure I knew Simon. 'bout as well as anyone ever
              knew him."

In the replay the catch was made three times.
And it didn't look harder.
And it didn't look easier.

When I had tried to find Simon's sister,
the only living relative, down in the City,
Everyone had responded with fear.

His sister had moved
His sister had died
What had she done
Who was I,   asking

Now if Walters had nothing to say,
I had nothing.

But Walters ordered another beer.
I bought us each a shot.
Maybe Walters would want to talk —

He had kept score for the game, the masterpiece,
and from what the warden said,
Simon had saved his life.

After a rally of sorts the Tiger reliever
Quieted everything down.
The bar was filling up. Walters nodded and yelled
to men as they came in.

Shadows crossed the big wall.
The bar's darkness, the green of the diamond
Held me.

Bill Walters smiled, even as his head bobbed.
It was a muscle spasm, kind of, a tic, and it was
fear, visible on his body —

All it had left to move.
"You shoulda seen him. Simon was the man.
 I tell ya, you shoulda seen that boy throw."

The prison's records listed:
Simon McCarter, Age 24, 6'5", 195 pounds,
              male, Negro
          incarcerated for Armed Robbery.

Age 24 was when he died.

"The best right-handed pitcher I ever saw."

I waited to find out who else he'd ever seen.
The Yankees lost the game.
They were laying back, playing passive baseball,
And they lost the game.

Bill Walters and I played a game of
electric darts —
Bill Walters, head bobbing, had the timing down,
and beat me badly.

Simon had been dead now for about fifteen years.

I walked the diamond
Simon's prison's yard
one September afternoon

        watched a prison team
        play a neighboring prison
        one steamy August

I kept watch on the shadow the wall made

            what an outfielder would
            need to know, deal with

I walked the diamond

        ran in from deep center
        ran down the line

        tested the grass, the holes, the rocky places

        near the wall,
            and they told me only three balls
            made it that far all afternoon

        near the wall
            I slammed against the wall

        running back,
            I jumped
                I lunged and fell

I stood on the mound and ran to cover a play at first

I watched where bunts would trickle in the grass

            I played his game out
            out by out

the ground that Franklin had to cover at short for both those plays

the hard-packed infield that he dove on for one great game-saving stop

I walked and walked that whole field looking at ruts and rises
small things that could have/did not change the perfect   from perfect

and I did
what he could not do

I walked back out
            into the world

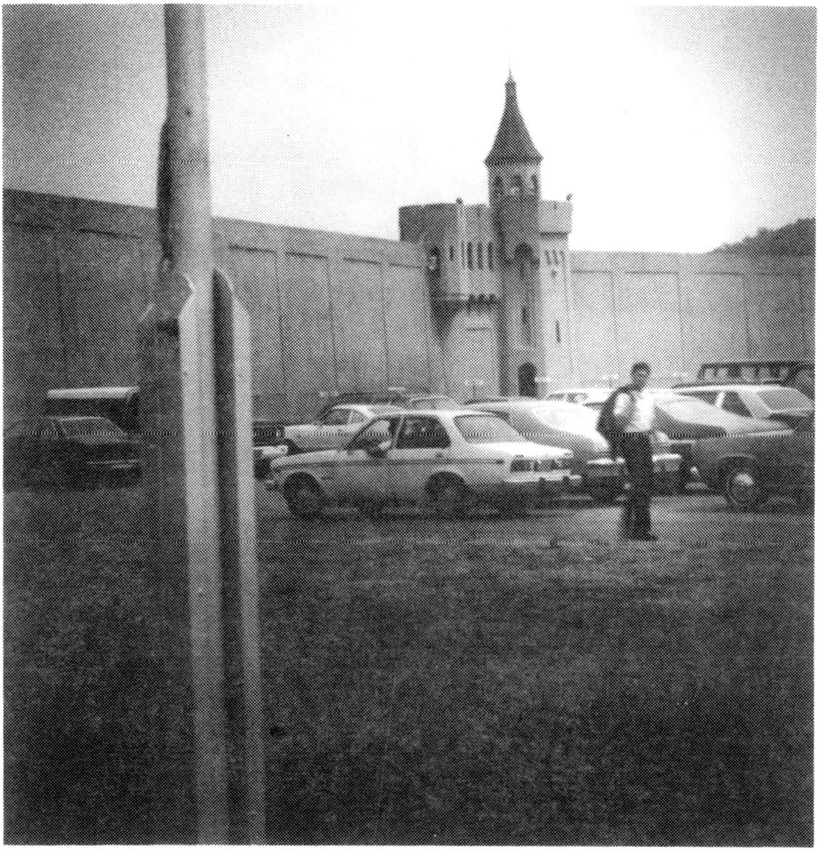

What Sam Porter liked about baseball
was the teams, the balance, the trades and races,
and how you could watch a team change slowly
over some years, see the whole character of the team
shift.
   Sam had seen so many games,
written so many up,
       followed so many teams, travelled with them,
that the joys of the single game
bright afternoon and just this diamond,
had lessened for him —

though when they were in the press box
Sam still seemed to be caught up in the moment.
His careful notations on his scorecard.

I watched each game.
Tried to keep each one separate, couldn't.
But those hardly visible shifts
which changed teams, and the whole sport
shifts in style, attitude, the very vision of the game,
hardly mattered to me.

Sam hated artificial turf, and didn't much like
night games — though I always chalked the latter up
to old age.
     He used to tell me about
     the bull-dozed old ballparks.

Day to day, in sunlight or under the lights
    I'd watch each game
    as if it was the only game,
          somehow special.

And too many were not.

Sam would yell across the other typewriters,
    "Waddaya writin' kid? A novel?
    There wasn't anything good enough to write
    that much about, kid.
    Just a bunch of guys tired after a long road trip,
     and one decent play by that centerfielder, out against
      the wall."

Sam was right.

The ballgame on the radio made the ride easier.

The files on the prisoners
and the files on the guards
are separated by a small table,
a chair, and a lamp.
They are on the same wall.
They are the same grey.
The files on the guards
only take up one cabinet.

It was the third inning
Franklin dove

stretched and reaching
fully extended

leapt from
the balls of his feet
at the crack of the bat

two steps to his left
and leaned across the dirt

Franklin dove

across the dusty, rock-hard basepath
to snag the ball

Simon turned to Franklin
dusting himself off
rubbing his shoulder, struck when he had rolled

reaching, snagged the shot
caught in mid-air, in silence
no friend of Simon's
caught and rolled

shoulder slammed and pulled, rolling
on the rock-hard field
                        came up grinning

Franklin dove
cat-quick and without even thinking
caught the ball and came up smiling

dove
Simon turned
to him
batter kicked his bat away
Simon
turned back
pitched

Simon listened, no one said anything,
 in that silence, Simon pitched
he pitched and grunted, the ball
slammed into the mitt, crackled in the August air.

Simon listened, a transistor radio
 in a guard tower, was loud enough
 for him to hear.
Someone in the outfield was humming along.
Simon listened, no crowd roaring, no let up,
 no getting off this mound
 until all these cons were out.

Mackintosh rattled bats together,
 picked the big one —
fuck him, Simon grunted to himself.

Simon listened, grunted, pitched
 in that silence.
In the guard tower — joking, laughter
 sound sinks here.
Simon remembered
 sounds: Saturdays on the street
 on the street when he was free
 walking with his friends, transistor radio
 blaring.

Jackson spit, pounded his bat
 in the dirt
                              psyche job —
fuck him, too, bastard.

pitching, getting them all out, listening,
 no one cheered.

In that silence, repeating what was
 perfect —
motion all one straining, grunting
 motion.

Simon listened, in that silence
 you could hear Hernandez's cut
 ripple the air

 in close, out on the corner
 bust em in
 tight on the hands

"Sure he claimed he was innocent, they all do."

I felt like I was in the middle of a bad prison movie
with the warden giving me the line.

"I didn't really get to know McCarter all that well.
He served his time. He was a quiet prisoner."

The term "model" seems to have gone out of the vocabulary.
He doesn't look me in the eye.

"About that game, well, you know how legends start.
You know the kind of myth-making, the hero syndrome
these men fall prey to..."

"But there are people still alive who saw the game..."

"There are more people alive who were in the stands when
Bobby Thomson hit his homerun, than could possibly have
fit into the Polo Grounds."

"Are you saying that Simon didn't pitch that game,
that you know it's a fabrication, and that some of
your own guards believe, and in fact, foster the lie..."

"Young man..."

He got up. I didn't mean to antagonize him.
I needed the files the prison had available. I needed names,
needed to be able to come and go in the prison.

"Young man, you seem to think that all of this makes a difference,
that for some reason, one dead black man, who pitched a fluke
of a game is somehow special."

I didn't want to think this, say this, but it bubbled out, the
expedient thing to say,

"Maybe not the man, but the game. Certainly the game was important."

It was exactly what he needed to hear.
I was a sports reporter again, and he had nothing to fear.
He sat back down and opened the files.

His sister, finally, the quiet afternoon in Brooklyn,
had taken out the pictures of her brother, of Simon,
had talked to me, reluctantly, suspiciously —
she wanted me to care about Simon, and I wanted to

but here was the bargain, the key, struck on the basis of
the game itself.
It had to be.

"Let me explain. No prisoner is a special or a significant man
when he is a prisoner. If he dies while he is in here, or if all
the people who know him on the outside die while he is in here,
and we let him out, leaving his only friends, his only human contacts,
behind this wall —
well, he is anonymous.   He is nothing.

"He has broken the law, and we are punishing him for it.
Rehabilitate, perhaps, but we are not a proving ground for his manhood.
I know too many widows of too many guards whose lives were taken as a measure
of that manhood.

"We   are in the business   of taking it   away."

He was glad, saying that, that I had no tape recorder, and that
I was just a sports reporter. It made all the difference in the world.

In the motel that night I read, listened to the Mets on the radio,
Seaver, not sharp, roughed up by the Pirates — all first ball hitting,
and wrote a piece about a season without Al Kaline. Went to bed.

His sister didn't believe me. Threw the book down, and told me to leave.
The sidewalk in Brooklyn was hot, and there were children out, all
over the streets.   I didn't know if she should believe me or not.

The old-timers at the office laughed the story off.
The editor didn't even say a word.

This warden, well, he might even get to thinking
about the story as a way to help him through the
penal system's bureaucracy.

A magazine I had requested was on my desk.
It was put out by the federal penal system, and had
an article about the psychology of sports in prisons.
I had expected it to start, something like, "short of
saltpeter, the best way of controlling caged men..."
It didn't start like that.
It started with a guard asking,
"What the hell is there for these guys to win, anyway?"
Dumb and obvious, right?
But a good question.

The Mets had lost three straight, and were coming home for a spell.
I called his sister, and asked her if she would like to see
a game, and she surprised me,   by saying yes.

Hernandez was playing too deep.

The ball wasn't going that far, and
    the infielders would never make it.
But Hernandez, from the sound of contact
    was running in.
And he wasn't graceful, or fast or even
    really a very good fielder.
But as the ball was on its way down,
    he jumped into the air,
like one of them Mexicans in Acapulco
    diving their swan dives off the cliffs
and the ball was in his mitt before he
    hit. Dust and rocks and gravel on
    his chest.
              He yelped.

It's the kind of game you win
because somebody's mistakes
don't cost you.

The fat boy jumping off the pier for
tourist money.
               The swan-diving
               Mexican
who runs like a bull.

Plays over his head.

some of the guys
the rip they took at Simon's pitch

that wall was everything they cared about
and everything they needed to defeat

that defeated them

About the sixth inning a wind came up
and dried the sweat on Simon's face;
but blowing out, and hard to predict,
he needed to bear down. He rocked and
pitched. He lurched out of memory on
that mound, cursing the wind, and fighting
it. Bearing down, and giving no ground,
he stopped them. Each con swinging
with the wind, at the wall, sat back down.

They hated him there that day. They hated
him like the wall. They hated him like
the screws. They hated him and battled him,
and no one gave up, and only Simon won.
Each batter knew that Simon was the only
one who could win this game. In the sixth inning
a wind came up, blew dust in their eyes, swirled,
caught one or two of them thinking —
with this to help, with this, catching it just right
got a shot at the wall. Get it over that fuckin'
wall. Show this Simon what I can do.

About the sixth inning a wind came up.
The outfielders moved, watched the clouds
moving fast; knew they'd get less now, because
he was bearing down, but knew that what they got would
be in the wind, would want that wind, and live there.
They knew that now the game was their's —
their's and the wind's.

About the sixth inning, from the guard tower,
one man looked down at the game. The stillness
of the diamond. The ferocity of the man on the
mound, grunting there. Looked down at the dust
swirling in patterns and falling back,
on this poor field. Watched one man on a mound,
buck everything, even the wind, and grunting,
throwing,   kick up his own dust.

he wonders if, perhaps,
the warden thinks of Simon's Masterpiece
as an anti-social act

what masks as triumph on the outside
what men assert over one another,
becomes the source of friction
on the inside

he is not, one guesses,
supposed to beat his fellows

but what is losing worth to anyone?

there is no seventh inning stretch
this is no sunday outing
beer and hot dogs in the stadium
cars parked out in the lot, windows open
hoping there'll be no rain, no robbery
this is no sunday outing
there is no seventh inning stretch
they play, sweat, run, watch, curse,
with the intensity of the damned

they are the damned
the game is no game here for them
sometimes, like today for Simon
it is the one way that they can
be stronger, better, wiser
sometimes, a ball clears the fences
and everyone's imagination of it
rolling free in the grass, is like a gasp
sometimes, running like murder to catch one
near the wall, at the warning track
the warning is something more than
simply   - wall approaching

ridiculously, the guard leans down
and you look up and he has you
in the sights of his gun, and
you are running ridiculous, playing a game
and risking death - the stupidest
death you could imagine
you jump near the wall and catch the
ball   and he puts his gun back down when
you turn and fire it in

sometimes, you catch the dude going into
second, pick him off from way out there
and the guard smiles down at you, always
goddamn it, down at you

the water bucket is covered with
a layer of dust, of bugs, and no one
wants to drink from it

and sometimes, Simon looks down from
the mound, looks like some kind of
avenging angel -   fires in there
beats you, beats you

that dumb nigger with his stretch
and kick and fire - magic
with his blazing eyes
and blazing fastball

you dream about the day he buys it
and you can start to hit again
dream about the fucker dying
when all that's dying is the game

bored and broken-spirited
men sit down, swearing
shouting - sometimes, really
other days, the fucking ball made it out -
got there - out into the world

you yell out to him
raise a fist, think about picking up a bat
and the guards look down
it isn't worth dying over
the fucker won't live forever

but what does live forever -
sometimes, you see the ball
past you, again and again
humiliating, stupid, and him,
black bastard, up there, beating you

he jams you, knuckles so sore
and stinging that you plunge your hand
into the bucket, through the
scum of spit now, dust and bugs,
move your hand and flex it, make a fist -
that hurts,

and pull it out, dripping
aching
sit right down on the ground
right there, shaking, furious

Simon and the screws, smile down at you
beaten.

Simon was in no hurry.
And they let him walk
    slow.
It wasn't that he wanted
    to stay there
    on that diamond
        forever.
It wasn't even that the
    life of the prison was so grim
    compared to the winning.
All it was
was one man walking
off a diamond
and back to his cell
            complete, at peace
            and silent, slow
            his own pace.

In a place where you walk as fast as you're told,
Walking slow is a defiant act.
Winning is a dangerous one.

Walked.

Simon dropped onto his bed.
    The coarse blanket brushed his arms,
    the one so tired, aching
    that he could almost believe he was still out there:

pitching, tensed and bearing down, sweating and battling,
    winning and pitching, showing all of them,
pitching

When I wake up
I know that it's gone

even pitching it
watched it slip away
nothing happened
I *kept* anything from happening

pissed it away
sometimes I wonder if I'll ever
have anything
something I can hold onto

and they walked us all back
to our cells
a muttering, shuffle of a walk

we showered and ate and watched t.v.
went to sleep when they turned out the lights
like every other day

like every other night

When I wake up
I know it's gone

one asshole   shouting like a fuckin' monkey
in his cage, shoutin' that
today he's gonna get me
today he's gonna rip one right by me

all strikeouts and groundouts yesterday
everything on the ground
but today, already, he's all mouth

like he was so pissed he spent the night
dreaming about it

and some guys
at breakfast
their jaws set, a little look over at me, like
it's done, man
you've had your day

and I can see in their eyes
that they're watchin' the ball
waitin' for the ball
even now
at breakfast

Sometimes I wish I could laugh

at all of them
Sometimes I wish I could break their
fuckin' necks
I can pitch
and sometimes I can even fool them

Sometimes
Yesterday
I can even fool myself

When I wake up
I wake up in the dark
before the lights come, stinging, on
before they wake us

It was only, really at Porter's funeral
that he realized that no one would ever print
Simon's story.

Porter had known that all along.

He wanted to throw the baseball into
the grave, and be done with it all.

A stupid thought, gesture.

He didn't say a word to anyone.

Porter's laughter, from death,
hung in the air around him.

A hollow and ferocious laughter that
he couldn't shake.

Laughter like the laughter at the end of
The Treasure of Sierra Madre

and his hands went slack
then tightened quickly
trying
just to feel
something

in the rain, outside the prison
he waited

this story had gone on too long
too many people, too much time
this one man's triumph had become something else
and, truthfully,
he was tired of it

tired of the bleakness, the backwards catch-22 humor of it
tired of the stupid cons and stupid screws
tired of a ballfield that never grew any grass
tired of this upstate landscape, and
    people in diners people in bars people in drugstores
    who never read novels
tired of their shitty small town newspapers, of having to
    pay more for the Times

and he was tired of his own attempt to spin it all into
    some kind of epic
a story that would grow beyond the pure physical masterpiece
into an encompassing drama
tired of failing with cripples and cons and black men and
    strong women and newspapermen, to breathe any life
    in
tired of the diamond and the perfection sucking it all dry

he was a sports reporter waiting in the rain outside the prison
whiskey on his breath and the flask in the glove compartment
chilled and up too early
he was
waiting for the catcher to be released
no one else would be coming for him   would give them time
    to talk

he remembered Parker's laughter echoing down the prison
halls, as the catcher had told him, that first day they talked,
    "I was catching him all day — and y'd think after
    all that —
        y'd think I could hit him
        — no chance. it was one of those days when you know
        what's coming and you still can't get hold of it,
        I couldn't,
            and I knew —
        lot a good knowing's ever done me,"
and the laughter grew in the halls, harsh and bitter as a cup
    dragged across the bars

he pushed it out of his mind as Parker came out of the prison
and into the world, and the rain
looking like a man who might not laugh, even that bitter, overloud
echoing laugh, ever again
Parker walked in the rain, slowly
he beeped for Parker to see him
Parker looked at the sky, didn't look back at the wall
in slow motion, came over to the car, and climbed in

he opened the glove compartment, and pointed to the flask
Parker's eyes laughed
                      while his hands went for the flask
one small mouthful
                      and he let it warm him, enter him, take
                      him by surpirse
                                  slow and warming as this rain
Parker put the flask back
and they drove off
away from the prison

"y'know — I was thinking about it. somewhere in the seventh
and eighth, the power guys all started trying
just to punch the ball, nobody was swinging for the
wall after awhile. y'd get up there and think   meet the ball,
just put it by somebody. it was kinda like the wall
closed in on us. ole Simon glaring down.

"y'know, he didn't smile much, not ever, and maybe not even once
during the whole game."

they thought of eating at the Hacienda, but it had closed down.

they put miles between themselves and the prison.

Parker's clothes were too new and too plain.

one diner had two state trooper cars in its lot, they decided
to skip that one — Parker kept watching everything —

"Simon didn't have friends. he wasn't that kind of dude.
you knew him — he let you know he was watching you.
didn't say much.

"but when he got the power guys to play his game. I knew
it was his game. my knees stopped aching — I coulda caught him
forever."

the Two Oaks diner was almost empty.   one waitress
was filling the sugar bowls and changing from the breakfast
menu to the lunch menu.   she brought them a morning paper
to look at.

no one looked over at them.
no one noticed how tired he was. how free Parker was.

they ordered.

the sun was coming out

When he told me, Parker did, passing by
the mansion with its gate and high fences,
that day in the rain, that morning before either
of us had eaten, when he told me that
that was the warden's house,
I laughed. A prison joke.
    Memory of a life they'd never have,
    glimpsed, one last sight,
    on their way in.

Weeks later, I laughed again.
When I found out it was the warden's house.
A prison joke.

The men in their greys
raked the leaves
but only
in the backyard.

and after lunch
we drove six hours
I asked Parker where he wanted
to go, and he didn't really know
decided on Boston
I had nothing else to do
we drove six hours
the rhythm of the road
the slow clearing of the day
and Simon, part of why we were
there together in that car

talked it through, three or four times
through the Berkshires
into the twilight, gathering

finally he said, quietly
"it's not something you ever forget"

and I wondered, looking at him
in the front seat
if that triumph, not his, not one bit
his triumph
somehow made him stronger now, here

when he got out of the car in downtown
Boston
and we said goodbye
I knew, saw, that it hadn't made him
strong enough

he stood there in the swirls of city
as I drove off
Parker laughing, Parker squatting down and catching,
Parker a party to this perfection, Parker caught
in a kind of a dream,   Parker — free

at the street corner
as the streetlights came on

in six hours with Simon with us
we had not talked about Parker
about tomorrow, about who he was
once he told me about a homer he had hit off Simon
and rounding the bases and Simon watching him
rounding the bases

and in the evening traffic
I knew that I was
wandering   too

tired of driving
I found myself parking, getting out of the car,
stretching
and walking around
darkened Fenway Park

I climbed a fire escape
with a sudden desperate desire to see
that diamond
reached a roof, and then, climbing up the billboard
where I had so often seen people gathered, watching
found that place and from that perch,
I looked out at the field

it was quiet, hollow, dark
and I felt foolish up there
looking

it was a ballpark I loved, but empty
and I was a little cold, the flask still
down in the car, in the glove compartment

I climbed back down
called an old friend to ask for a place to stay
got back to the car
which had a ticket on the windshield

I crumpled it up and drove away
turned on the Sox on the radio
and got lost twice on the way to my friend's

them times,   he leaned into the pitch
angrily, and thought about
them times -
when these same cons caught one just right
and knocked it over the wall
and rounded the bases laughing
like they was free

he leaned into the pitch
rocked and dealt
swing and miss
               and only he was laughing now

laughed like they had won something
laughed like they was free
Simon knew there wasn't much to win
and no way to follow the damn ball
on out, over the wall

smoked it in there, caught the corner
brushed them back, knocked McGuire
on his ass
        who'd laughed his ass off
        last week
        rounding the bases

this time, nobody was gonna fuck him over
this time, watched each one walk away
muttering, mad, and shaking their fists
this time, he'd show them something

the wall pressing in on his shoulders
leaning against him
bearing down on him
as he went into his wind-up

all them fucking times
they thought they had him
suckers smashing a white ball over a grey high wall
and fooled into thinking they was free

perfect   on this diamond
throwing all I am at them
like   spitting in their faces

like splitting their dreams open

this is for all them times
them times is over
today

the ball popped in Parker's mitt

They cannot win.
They know they cannot win
Behind me, backing me up, out in the field
       for the last three outs
there's not a thing they can do
but lose it for me.
              And there's no fucking way
I'll let them lose it for me.

Looking at each of them, around the infield,
I think they know it.
If anybody's gonna get a hit, it's gonna come off me.
Nobody's gonna hang onto one too long, nobody's gonna
       throw one into the dirt, or let one play them.
       Nobody's gonna get one caught in the webbing.
Nobody who wants to live
       is gonna make that kind of mistake —
They know it.

And if they're angry, slammed their bats down in their last ups,
       and yelled,
If they're furious with themselves, with me, still muttering
       under their breath, looking out at the mound
       at me —
let them use that anger.
              Let them make that anger make that throw.

I start Willie Jones off with one way outside.
One that slips away from me, one that's forced
       from my aching arm.
What about the anger that uncorks one, wild?
       The anger that could lose it for me,
       no edge.
              Keep the ball away from hotheads.

The outfield's too far off. There's no way to glare them
       into line. In their own little world out there
       and no way to make them afraid.
       There's too much they cannot know, each one
              alone in the shadow of the wall.

In the infield, it's like you're chained together. And when it works
       even on this rocky, brokedown diamond,
       when each one moves and watches and is ready
       and cannot win
              but plays
              better than they ever could
              behind me —
       I pitch.

Willie swings at one and misses.

Off to one side, Ron Murphy's yelling something.
Almost the only sound.

Willie's fast enough, and slaps the ball around.
The rocks and holes all work for him here.
    You run in on a trickler off Willie's bat
    and it tricks you
             hits a rock, runs right up your arm,
             all the funny bounces
    and Willie's fast enough.

Murphy's got the bat away from Miceli
    and swinging and yelling in front of the bench.
It's pissing Willie off.
It's pissing everybody off. And taking time.

When Willie finally connects he slaps one at
    Jackson at third, who has to charge it.
I hit the deck, and lying on my stomach
    in the dirt, I have to watch it all:

Willie quick out of the box
the fucking ball slowing down
Jackson who shouted before, bat tossed away, he'd get me,
           coming in on it, and off balance
           arcing his throw to first.

Me, I'm on my stomach, spitting, thinking
that's it, the whole fucking ballgame, just
because Jackson skies one,   even when I know
off-balance,   that he had to.

Mackintosh, at first, is ready. Smooth as silk
he makes the play, beats Willie by about a step.

And Willie argues, glares at Murphy.
I look at Jackson and at Mackintosh.
Slap the dust from my shirt
and Murphy comes to bat.

Took the bat from Miceli, poor fucked-over Miceli,
and came to bat.

Even the outfielders are interested in this one.
Pig shaking his fist at me and wagging his ass in the box.
But with everyone behind me,
This one's mine.

striking out Murphy
getting him to swing at bad pitches
making him look like an asshole

and all the cons laughing in his face
giving him shit
because he thought, that late in the afternoon,
bat in hand, that he was gonna break it up

Murphy, who'd break your arm as soon as look at you
Murphy, a guard with scars and a kid and some guys said,
a pretty wife
Murphy, who'd stick his elbow in your face in basketball
all winter long, until he got you mad
Murphy, who you couldn't hit back

white, pale, straining and battling
batting to break it up,
Murphy went for one way down in the dirt
swung too hard, too late for another one

face red, spitting, teeth tight with his anger
he fouled a couple off
kicked at the dirt and set himself
concentrated, and then, frowning
gritting like this one pitch would mean
everything

missed it completely, twisted around
and swore in the dust
as all the cons shouted and laughed and
waited for him to throw the bat down
snarl, stare them all down,
to make them shut up

Murphy stalked out of the box
and looked back out at the mound
at Simon

Murphy looked out at me
and swore, making a fist

I threw him what I threw
because of who he is
because, flailing and chopping and spun around
he looked like an asshole

I had wanted to talk to Murphy
Parker had mentioned him
Everyone hated him
He seemed, in a funny way, striking out there,
    the next to last out in the ninth
like a pivotal figure
and somehow, like an intrusion, a threat
    to the game, like the cloud in the second:

I tried to figure out if it was because his stake
in all of it was higher
or if that strikeout was just the last grunt
before the easy pop-up

I tried to understand why a man would risk
so much, just to stand up there,
so late in the afternoon
just to prove himself

I tried to figure, the man who broke Jack's jaw
why he needed to get at them this way too, bat in hand
and how he failed

His wife, skinny, kind of pretty, looked away
    asked me not to bother them, went back to arranging
    small toys on the shelves of the store

    it was sweltering in the store, and the large fan
    swirling the air for the ceiling, made it no cooler

    I mopped my forehead with a handkerchief
    I didn't want to bother her

    she didn't want questions
    didn't want to remember

She was who was left
    Walters had told me
    how Murphy'd been the first one killed
    in the riot

    and even Walters said how much they'd hated Murphy

    the man who broke Jack's jaw

his wife said
    "Ronnie never hurt anybody in his life."

in this whole goddamn
wall-burdened town
on both sides of that wall

there was never anyone who was guilty

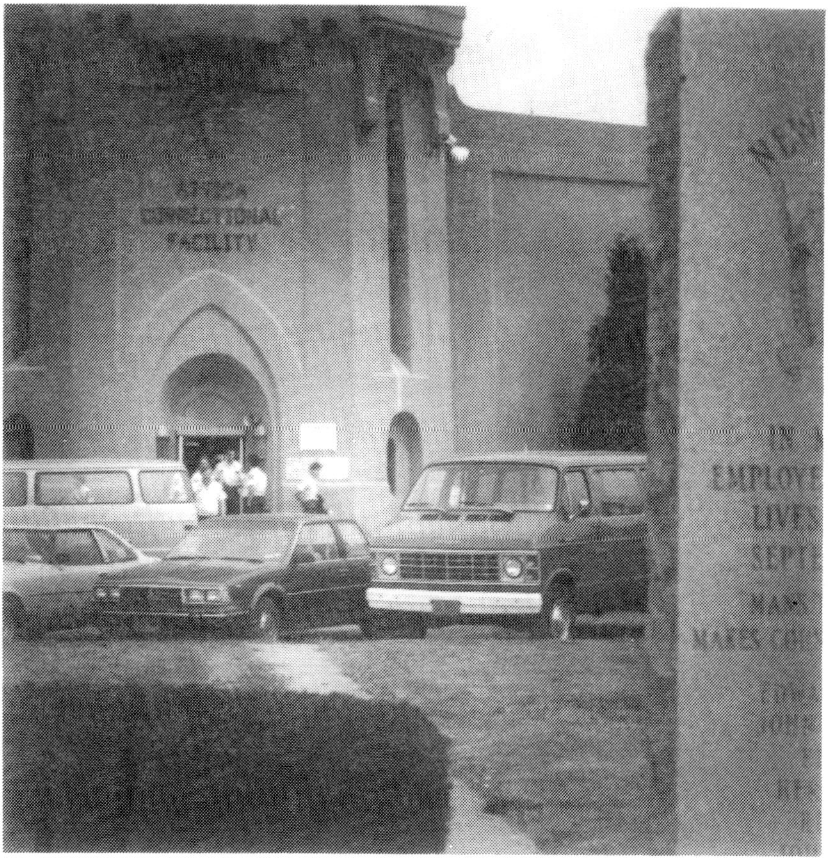
ATTICA
CORRECTIONAL
FACILITY

because of who he was

Janet Murphy came out of the store
with a group of friends, closing time
all talking and laughing

she saw me waiting, and sent them off
down the hill without her

"I told you I don't have anything to say."

Ron Murphy had played football
for a nearby high school.
He hadn't grown up in town.

They had one son.

We walked down the hill.
Janet Murphy told me more about him.

"Why do you want to know about Ronnie?
 Nobody really cares what happened to him.
 Town's full of widows."

Her voice flattened against these words
all emotion, all bitterness, almost all memory
gone from it

"It isn't really Ronnie I'm asking about..."

"If it's for one of them niggers they got locked up in there,
 you better just leave me alone, now."

"It isn't about anyone really, just something that happened,
 something important, a long time ago. Did he ever talk about them?"

"He'd come home sore, y'know. He'd come home and have a couple
 beers, and mutter some about it. But he never talked about
 anybody in there."

Jonathan ran across the lawn to his mother. Hugged.
She put him between us. I shook his hand, and listened
as they talked about school.

We continued, through back streets, down the hill
and closer to the prison.

Their apartment, over a grocery,
was small. They had a big t.v. and almost no books.
Magazines on the coffee table.

Jonathan went into his room to do homework.
Janet started making dinner,
She looked up and asked,

"Did you want to stay for dinner?"

"No, thanks, really. I have to get going."

Sad small gestures with no feeling and no response.
I had nowhere to go, except my motel room, a diner somewhere.
She had asked only because I was standing there.
Neither of us said anything.

Ronnie Murphy was dead.
Simon McCarter was dead.
Sam Porter, who threw me the ball
    in the City, was dead.

Janet Murphy moved through her kitchen.
Had met Ronnie many years before.
Got used to living in this town with its wall.

Got used to, slowly, a world without Ronnie
coming home, sore, from the prison.

And finally, got used to Jonathan, growing up,
looking like Ronnie.

I picked up my coat, off the back of the chair,
and noticed the picture on the wall.

"That's Ronnie, and the car."

He smiled out of the picture, a shit-eating grin
standing there in front of his stock car, wearing prison greys
and holding a cloth and a can of wax.

"Did he wear those often, the greys?"

"The what... oh, those, they're just something
he brought home one day.
Ronnie loved that car."

"Did he take her out to the track?"

"Once and a while, but Ronnie liked to win, y'see.
And we just didn't have enough money to put into her."

I nodded and looked back at Murphy's face.
Said goodnight to Jonathan, in his room, at the books.
From his window you could see rooftops, and one guard tower.

"I don't like to remember so much. I try not to."

"I know. I'm sorry, really."

The dinner smelled good.

I came looking for pain or anger or tears

and found this silence.
I wanted to know if Ronnie Murphy had risked everything
because of who he was,
And ended up having to ask if it was because of who he was not,
could not be.

I looked for him, maybe even the way that
Simon McCarter pitched him —
pushing a little too hard, risking a little too much.
Looked for him special, important, somehow
separate from the rest,

And in this small apartment
found this picture of his car and him,
with his shit-eating grin.

A real s.o.b.

Coming down the hill
she told me how, sometimes,
when there are problems inside,
the tear gas catches the wind,
and the whole apartment is unbearable.

She told me how, crying, and holding
handkerchiefs to their faces,
they had gone back up the hill
to stay with friends.

They were beginning to know me at
this diner.
It didn't feel like home.
Anybody's.
But I had tried others, with their
home-cooking, and their specials.
The food filled you up here.

When I got back to the motel
after dinner, there was a note.
Walters was down at Tony's,
and he wanted to speak to me.

it ends as somebody pops to me
Parker smiles about this
the Connecticut River meanders by us
the Pike in golden light

he has gone through the game three times now
and this is the first time he's told me this part
what he owns of the game
it ends as somebody pops to me

I squeeze the ball
and look out to Simon
can't really say anything at all to him

it doesn't go on forever, forever
or until someone scores
it's not that kind of game
it goes nine innings, and then it's done

they march us back to our cells

in a high sky I watch it
I call for it, wave the third baseman off
I see it go to the top of its flight
touch sky, get caught like a lump in the throat of the sun
and then, start back down

it's hard to see and hard to judge
my legs shift under me
I circle under it
I freeze, lock, watch, and catch the ball
in the silence

look out to Simon
flip the ball to him
it's really his now
and say nothin'

the Connecticut valley is warm
car windows wide open
and Parker smiles over this
what he tells me last, what is his

yeah, I throw the mask off first,
it's a reflex, I didn't tell ya 'bout it
'cause I just do it, far enough so that I won't
trip over it,   and then I run
fighting the sun, looking up into the sun
watching it come down
into my glove, and hardly even breathing
until I squeeze the thing in my glove
and it's over

Tony's was packed.
Guys watching Monday Night Football.
Tarkenton picking apart a defense.
Guys I recognized, guards from the prison.

Walters was in his corner.

I pushed my way through.

Walters shouted,
"Goddammit, get over here."

For a while, driving in from the motel,
I had thought that something might have broken
the lock Walters had on all those memories.

He had told me so little.
And every time I thought he had something
to tell me, it slipped away.

Tonight he was furious.
Scowled at me,

"I *thought* I *told* you to leave her alone."

"Look, I'm really sorry, but I needed to talk with her."

"You needed to! Tell me about it.
Don't you know how many people in this town
walk around with scars? Don't you know by now
how much it hurts here?
How much people *need* to be left alone, to be able to
forget, survive?
           And you, you're real sorry
           but you needed..."

"Listen..."

"No, you listen to me!"

A few guys near our table had turned from the game.
For the first time in months here, I felt afraid.
And for the first time with Walters, it felt like
          maybe I had touched a nerve.
People moved in closer around us.

"Now you listen good. Don't you even care?
Ron Murphy was a bastard. I'll say it. If anybody had it coming
it was that sonofabitch.
But he was one of us.

We never asked for them to cage their garbage up
in our town. But they did it,
and Ron Murphy, and a whole lot of other guys died
inside there.

And some of 'em,   didn't even get to die.

And it isn't o.k. with us for you to use your fuckin' angel,
your goddam perfect pitcher, to make us all look like pigs.

You didn't *know* Simon. He was one mean black bastard.
He'd look through you. He wouldn't say a fuckin' word, and
He'd watch you.

Sometimes you'd just want to gouge his eyes out.
You'd just want to hit him 'til he screamed,
And he'd just stay quiet.
Big dumb buck quiet. Fucking animal quiet. Like you didn't even exist.
Watching you."

Somebody in the corner laughed and shouted,
"If he hollers let 'em go."
And somebody else yelled,
"Hey, Bill, who's your niggerlover friend?"

Walter was done. His anger, confused and guilty anger,
was spent.   And he was free of it.
But it was ringing through the bar, rippling across
          small groups, shapes of people in the half-dark
          drinking and watching the game,
          watching the game and laughing.

Tarkenton saw everything on the field.
Looking at him, you could catch up on the game,
     get lost in it, to keep from looking
     at anyone.
You could guess the score, or close, by the way he moved.
Saw everything, tensely, waiting,
     always a threat to run.

"I'm sorry. I know there's a lot everybody'd like to forget."

No answer from him. Muttering.

A receiver, in that jittery dance with a cornerback
all the way down the side line
caught one, bobbled it a bit, and then made his move
and put on the speed.
Knees high, raced into the end zone.

"You're gonna owe me,"
A half-drunk voice called across the bar.
"It ain't over yet."

"Tell me about the game. I want to hear more about the game."

"Sure you do. You been saying a couple months now how it's the
game you're interested in, just the game.
You ever stop to think how that makes
all the people feel?"

"I've thought about it."

"Well I remember the whole fuckin' day.
And maybe I do because you been buggin' the shit outta me.
And maybe I just do."

We drank and talked.

"When we got off shift, we come over here
to Tony's, only Tony didn't own it then.
We come over here and nobody said a word.

I don't think any of us believed it."

When Tarkenton scrambles, it is so
much an escape from the lines and patterns
of the game, that everyone stops —
and all you watch is that lone figure
retreating and watching and eluding,
until someone gets free and he unloads
before anyone gets a hand on him.
A different excitement than the sound
of bodies slamming into the line, those bursts.

"And I remember that cloud that came over
in the second.
                Some of those mothers'll
                tell you,
you talk with them too,
don't you?"

His look was knowing, level, fierce.

"Some of them'll tell you how we used to
keep them out in the rain.

How we'd make 'em all get soaked and muddy,
get pneumonia, sometimes even frostbite.
They'll tell you that.

I guess some guys kept 'em out in the rain, sometimes."

The undercurrent of anger seethed
through the bar, surrounded me, pushed at me.

"In the second inning, there was this cloud.
Blew in across the diamond.
                                This was way before anybody had
any idea what was comin', what the day and the game were
gonna be.

The cloud came over, and we coulda all gone in
and it never woulda happened.

But it blew on by. Didn't rain. Probably poured
over in Syracuse.
And almost as quick as it came over, it was gone again,
and the whole sky was empty.

Lemme tell you, it's a helluva thing, when you're in there,
walls and cons all around you, and a big black cloud comes over
and sticks a lid on the place.
                            It's like choking."

Outside, in the October night,
a breeze with the beginning of winter in it
blew down the funnel of street the wall made,
picking up leaves and litter, rattling windows and
tipping garbage cans.

The dark bar was filled with noise.
The half-time highlights were met with
    hoots and cheers.
Someone shouted, "Turn off the sound, that fuckin' Cosell
    makes me sick."
Someone else, laughing, "And change the channel before
    they show the goddam Giants."

"Did anybody say anything about the no-hitter
as it went along, or did they just keep quiet?"
"If you're talking about that superstition, 'bout it
jinxing the game to talk about it, shit, everybody talked
and swore and yelled and threatened,
and Simon threw that fuckin' ball like, almost like
he was all alone. Almost like he could've done it
any time he wanted.
                      Like nobody but him mattered."

"You think he could have?"

"Pitched it *any*time?
No fucking way. remember this, you're talkin' about
one dumb con with a good fastball and a lot of luck
and a day when he got all the breaks.

The next day they hit the living shit out of the ball.

He couldn't do it anytime he wanted, nobody could.
He wasn't no god."

At some point you know Fran is going to his tight end.
And you know that, a part of the blocking, suddenly the guy
   is going to slip through
                            and Fran is going to find him
                            open over the middle.
You know this, seeing it, you smile.
The defense knows it too. And the tight end is not that big
   or that fast —
                the pass is there.
                The first down they needed, they get easily.

"That Tarkenton is one tricky bastard."

And somewhere in the smothering darkness
I have gotten it confused.
I have mistaken their anger with Tarkenton:
tricky, getting away, changing their game of
crush and power, with his slippery moves,

with their anger with me:
who will not let them forget.

"Did you keep the score sheet from the game?"

"It was fifteen years ago, man. Waddaya think? I got it
   framed or somethin'?"

I can't tell if Walters has more to say.
I can't even tell if he's still mad, mad enough
   to send some guys out into the street
   after me.

Sam Porter always used to talk about the edge
that danger gave his work. Liked it.
I didn't buy that one, at least not here.
All I felt here was darkness, moving in shapes
   in the bar's crowd.

Somehow the whole town now was somehwere

where there'd be threats, where maybe I'd
have to replace slashed tires.

And if, trying to see their faces in the darkness,
I was tired of all of them, of this place,
this stifling little, propped-against-the-wall place
and all its ruined people,
well, maybe they were more than tired of me,
me and my questions.

"You didn't have to bother her."

He's made his point.

And maybe, in the diner,
the breakfast waitress, Ann, who knew me
from all these mornings,
wouldn't fill my cup a second time,
without her charging, without my asking.

I wondered what the guard tower looked like
at night, with the lights on,
from his window.

I wondered what he thought of it.

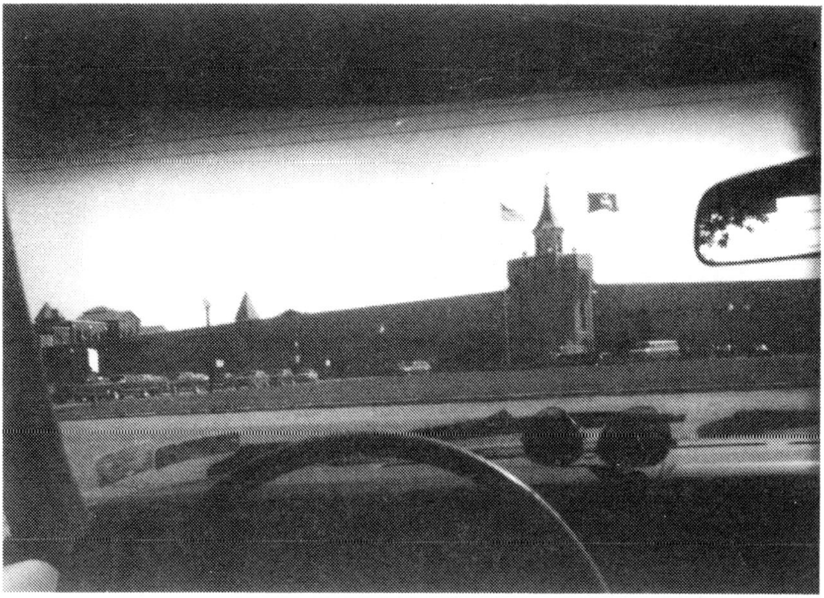

She didn't even look up. Poured him another cup.
And walked away.
He walked around the outside wall —
A new geometry, in morning light.
Sam Porter's wife wept into the phone.
He watched the series surrounded by lineups
    and a homemade scorecard,
in his room at the Sand Creek Motel.
She didn't charge for the second cup, joked with
    the hunters in the booth near the door.
It wasn't an exaggeration, how good everyone was saying
    the sixth game was.
Litter and weeds, broken glass, newspaper, all clung
    to the base of the wall,
    at least until the wind shifted.
High school kids had written in spray paint
    names, dates, numbers, challenges,
    boasts.
Paula had smiled and said, "that was before I had a phone,"
    when he asked about the telegram
    telling her that
    Simon was dead.
The wind shifted. Old newspapers caught at my feet.
    I shielded my eyes from grit.
It will be a good day to drive
    back to the City.

Hunters' cars on the roadside.
Their red jackets, the sound of their rifles.
Almost all the way home.

On the subway back to her apartment
Seaver on the mound kept flashing up in my eyes.
His patience. His power. His canny work there,
Pitching with all of his knowledge and memory and
        body brought to bear —
            not tricks,   but knowing.

In the apartment she put on some music and
        got me a beer.

I knew all along that Paula really didn't have that
        much to tell me, but it didn't keep
        the frustration from rising in me.
        A frustration I couldn't find any way of directing.

She smiled.
"You know you probably know more about him than I do.
 You're the one who talked to all the convicts and
        guards and people who knew him for all that time.
I just got letters.
I just outlived him.
            Lucky, I guess."

It was more than that, more than lucky, but she was right,
        she had so little to tell me.
        She had started out confused, a little frightened
            by my interest.
        I think she knew now how much the whole thing
            obsessed me
        and that frightened her.

She opened the album on the table.
"These are the letters."

His handwriting was careful, almost delicate, perhaps
        labored, and the phrases were not at all
        revealing. Nothing he wrote told me anything
        about him.

"It's funny, y'know, Simon never even said enough in his letters
  to get them censored. But he wrote pretty regularly."

Somehow, suddenly, it all seemed so long ago,
        in such a depth of past, that all of this
        effort, this digging, couldn't possibly

uncover it all.
And no one wanted.

So that's it, Porter, you old bastard —
The story without a center, with nothing to hang it on,
    with all these pieces and no way to
    fit them all together.

I tried to imagine what Simon looked like
    out there on the mound.

I talked to Paula about her life, and always back again
    to Simon.

"I can't help feeling it hasn't helped anyone.
Can't help feeling like somewhere here I got lost,
    and there's really no way out."

She looked at me, maybe surprised, or hurt:
"Think about it, about all you've told *me*."

I wasn't sure what she meant.
She coached the answer out of me,

"One day in a prison, and it doesn't even really matter where,
one man did something very special, something that had never
been done before, something that separated him from everyone else.
And then that day was over.
He was a prisoner.
He died.
Some people remember."

She looked at me, even, quiet,

"And some people are changed."
The dark town, wall, bar, anger, welled in me
and went away.
                      Parker whirled around through his freedom,
                      almost lost.

"Not just me, Andrew, but you too."
And wanted to lighten all of this, laughed
"You're not the scared honky who came up here a few months ago
asking all those questions."

I liked the way Paula laughed.

I tried to imagine what Simon looked like out there
    on the mound, the scar flashing on the side
    of his face, flaming.

I folded up the telegram and put it back in the envelope.

the kind of perfect
the kind of quiet
                       that leaves them

        shaking their heads